War Sports Embracing Grenade Throwing, Boxing, And Athletic Drills: Arranged In Accord With Military Procedure

F. L. Kleeberger

In the interest of creating a more extensive selection of rare historical book reprints, we have chosen to reproduce this title even though it may possibly have occasional imperfections such as missing and blurred pages, missing text, poor pictures, markings, dark backgrounds and other reproduction issues beyond our control. Because this work is culturally important, we have made it available as a part of our commitment to protecting, preserving and promoting the world's literature. Thank you for your understanding.

# War Sports Embracing Grenade Throwing, Boxing, and Athletic Drills, Arranged in Accord with Military Procedure

F. L. KLEEBERGER, B. S., M. A.

*Associate Professor of Physical Education, Director of Men's Gymnasium, and Director of Athletics for the School of Military Aeronautics, University of California, Berkeley, California*

AND

EARL H. WIGHT, B. L.

*Instructor in the Department of Physical Education and in the School of Military Aeronautics, University of California*

REPRINTED FROM
THE AMERICAN PHYSICAL EDUCATION REVIEW
MAY AND JUNE, 1918

# WAR SPORTS EMBRACING GRENADE THROWING, BOXING, AND ATHLETIC DRILLS, ARRANGED IN ACCORD WITH MILITARY PROCEDURE.

F. L. KLEEBERGER, B. S., M. A., ASSOCIATE PROFESSOR OF PHYSICAL EDUCATION, DIRECTOR OF MEN'S GYMNASIUM, AND DIRECTOR OF ATHLETICS FOR THE SCHOOL OF MILITARY AERONAUTICS, UNIVERSITY OF CALIFORNIA, BERKELEY, CALIFORNIA,

AND

EARL H. WIGHT, B. L., INSTRUCTOR IN THE DEPARTMENT OF PHYSICAL EDUCATION AND IN THE SCHOOL OF MILITARY AERONAUTICS, UNIVERSITY OF CALIFORNIA.

## INTRODUCTION.

The future must provide a new, broad and extensive physical education developed not alone through formal, disciplinary, corrective or educational gymnastic drill, not alone through athletics of the "bleacher" type, but through a comprehensive system of *physical drill, free play,* and *highly organized* athletics used for the development of real physical efficiency in our entire citizenry. To promote among the youth of the country the desire and ability to keep physically fit, the acquirement of respect for *discipline,* and the habit of "playing the game" hard, squarely and to win is sure to give us a soldier citizenry superior in fighting quality to any merely military-trained army in the world.

Upon the assumption that a man should be prepared to play a man's part in life from the standpoint of physical fitness as well as from the standpoint of intellectual attainment, and that the physical exigencies which a man might be required to meet could well be conceived as including fighting, swimming, and agility of a type calculated to safeguard him from accident and to stimulate his continued participation in health-giving sports, a system of physical efficiency tests[*] based on the above phases of training was established in 1915, by the Department of Physical Education for Men at the University of California.

---

[*] See Physical Efficiency Tests as a Method of Popularizing Physical Education at the University of California. AMERICAN PHYSICAL EDUCATION REVIEW, December, 1917, January, 1918.

Since the possibilities of disciplinary training through the processes of physical drills were recognized and appreciated, and since it was necessary to teach large groups of men certain muscular coördinations with their practical bearing, the formal method of class instruction was used wherever possible for the fundamental training in the desired coördinations. Experience has demonstrated that this method of formal procedure under proper direction is most efficient in developing skilled performers and is far superior to formal drills of the ordinary type, which lack *content as far as practical application* is concerned. Thus the men in boxing drills get equal disciplinary training with those in the classes of Swedish gymnastics, do more work than the latter, and possess a more practical physical ability as a product of their expenditure of time and effort.

The deadly thing about formal gymnastic drill has always been its *lack of content;* and it is in the effort to promote the use of formal drill with its peculiar values, and at the same time give it a natural interest—*a practical and appealing content*—that this manual of war sports is formulated.

The fact that the exercises included are presented in a standardized *formal* way should in no wise lead any one to think that a scheme of physical training should *confine* itself to the purely formal practice of these exercises. The practice of these drills should hold the significance in the process of physical education that the finger exercises and running of the scales hold in the training of the skilled pianist.

An outline of the complete organization of the athletic work for a school or small military camp is here exemplified in the plan formulated for the U. C. School of Military Aeronautics, which is seen to embrace "War Sports" as one of its elements.

In the carrying through of such work reference to Dr. J. H. McCurdy's treatise on athletic games, relay races, etc., for large groups of men in France, and to Dr. H. F. Kallenberg's mass athletics, will prove most helpful.

The authors of this manual are indebted to Mr. G. R. Kleeberger, Mr. Marcus Freed, Mr. M. H. Trieb, and Mr. Walter Christie for valuable assistance in the compilation of this material.

TENTATIVE ORGANIZATION OF ATHLETICS FOR THE SCHOOL OF

MILITARY AERONAUTICS, UNIVERSITY OF CALIFORNIA.

*General Statement.*

Athletic and recreative sports organized for the students of the School of Military Aeronautics at the University of California have been grouped according to the following schedule, with three objects constantly in mind as outlined by General Squier, chief signal officer of the army, in the curriculum for the United States Schools of Military Aeronautics, March 1, 1918.

*First,* so far as limitations of space and equipment make it possible, the recreative values of "informal sports" are developed. *Second,* the plan aims to systematically build up the "physical fitness" of every man, not alone as to health, strength, and endurance, but also as to specific ability in fighting, climbing, swimming, jumping and such other activities as will stand him in good stead in meeting the physical exigencies he may have to face. And, *third,* the effort is made through organization of interindividual, intersquad, and intersquadron competition to develop that "lively sense of esprit de corps," loyalty, and group interest which should be the motive force and joy of any fighting unit. Throughout the whole scheme an orderliness of procedure and an attention to military methods and discipline are constantly emphasized.

The organization of each phase of the work is divided into three elements: the formal, instructive, disciplinary phase; the informal, competitive phase—interindividual and intersquad competition; and the formal intersquadron competitive phase. Every Friday is given to formal intersquadron competition, the results of which are recorded, as is done in a baseball series. The percentage held by any squadron may thus be constantly figured and recognition given each squadron setting a new mark either in one type or in all six types of activity.

*Schedule.*

Squadrons A-B. Midfield and Harmon Gymnasium for a period of two weeks.

3.10–3.25—Dressing.
3.25–4.00—Boxing and wrestling drills.
4.00–4.15—Individual competition, each squad leader forming his squad into a ring and pitting the men against one another in rotation, grading each man upon his individual efficiency.
Each squad, through this process, will determine the two boxers who are to represent it in intersquad competition each day and the squadron in the weekly intersquadron competition during the combat tournament to be held each Friday afternoon.
4.15–4.30—Intersquad competition.
F. L. Kleeberger and M. Freed in charge.
4.30–4.50—Time allowed for bathing and dressing.

Squadrons C-D. West Field.

3.10–3.25—Dressing.

3.25–4.15—Agility training through "War Sports," such as grenade throwing, wall scaling, fence vaulting, etc., squad athletic leaders taking charge of squads in personal competition looking forward to intersquad and intersquadron competition in the Friday afternoons' "War Sports" tournaments. Competition will consist of five events: shelf scaling, rope climbing, twenty-yard run carrying an injured or helpless person, hand wrestling, and tug-of-war; efficiency of the individual to be graded by the squad leaders in consultation with the athletic instructors.
E. H. Wight and M. H. Trieb in charge.
4.15–4.30—Intersquad competition.
4.30–4.50—Time allowed for bathing and dressing.

Squadrons E-F. California Oval.
3.10–3.25—Dressing.
3.25–4.00—Track and field training. Groups should be kept in military units (squads, platoons, etc.) during the practice of running, jumping, hurdling, etc.
4.00–4.15—Individual competition within each squad, under the direction of the squad athletic leader will determine the representatives for intersquadron field and track meet based upon five events: high jump, broad jump, hand vault, grenade throw and 100-yard dash; efficiency grading of *each individual* by the squad leader in consultation with the athletic instructors.
Mr. Cozens in charge.
4.15–4.30—Intersquad competition.
4.30–4.50—Time allowed for bathing and dressing.

Squadrons G-H. California Field.
3.10–3.25—Dressing.
3.25–3.45—Squad leaders drill their men in "Westmoreland" and advantage wrestling.
3.45–4.30—Competition between intersquad and intersquadron teams in multiple soccer, softball baseball, group relay racing, obstacle racing, "over-the-top," pushball, "pivot the man," "pull away," "whip the Kaiser," etc.
F. W. Cozens in charge.
4.30–4.50—Time allowed for bathing and dressing.

*Squadrons I-K-L-M. Swimming Pool and Rifle Range.
3.00–3.25—Marching to the pool and dressing.

---

* Only two squadrons to be at the pool at any one time, the remaining squadrons alternating at the Rifle Range. For a period of four weeks: Squadron I, Monday, Wednesday, Friday, 3.00-5.00; Squadron M, Tuesday, Thursday, 3.00-5.00; Squadron K, Monday, Wednesday, Friday, 3.00-5.00; Squadron L, Tuesday, Thursday, 3.00-5.00.

3.25–3.45—Class drills in the principles of swimming, diving, resuscitation and rescue. Drills in the different strokes.

3.45–4.15—Individual competition within each squad as above, each man being graded by the squad athletic leader as to his ability in swimming, diving, and rescuing and selection made by the squad of the two men to represent them in the formation of the team for intersquadron competition.

4.15–4.30—Intersquad competition.

A. W. Dowden and S. T. Flynn in charge.

4.30–4.50—Dressing and returning to the drill grounds.

**Squadrons I-K-L-M. Traps or Rifle Range.

3.00–4.30—Trap shooting and rifle practice.

Intersquad and intersquadron competition.

## HAND-GRENADE THROWING.

The hand-grenade now in use for throwing practice at the Presidio at San Francisco, California, and therefore adopted for use at the University of California, is a cylindrical block of green eucalyptus wood, rounded at the ends, measuring some 6½ inches in length and 3 inches in diameter, and weighing approximately 350 grams.

The Mills grenade No. 5, weighing 600 grams, now largely used by the French, is approximately of the above dimensions; while the offensive grenades used by the French are about the size of a baseball and weigh only 250 grams.

The method of throwing with the arm straight is uniform for all types, however, and more typical of the English game of cricket than of American baseball. The chief reason for developing a straight arm throw is to protect the arm and shoulder from the snap of the baseball throw, which makes the latter method of throwing impossible with the heavy grenades. The straight arm throw is also conducive to the development of a proper trajectory, causing the grenade to describe an arc which allows it to drop more directly into a trench as an objective; and, in addition, this form in throwing is more conducive to the development of uniform results and is better suited to the cramped quarters obtaining where throwing is being done from the trenches.

Usually the grenades are thrown as a line of men advances on a trench, the purpose being to form a barrage, thus causing the enemy to keep their heads down and their guns out of use; they

---

**Only one squadron to be at the Rifle Range at a time. For a period of four weeks: Squadron I, Tuesday, Thursday, 3.00-5.00; Squadron M, Monday, Wednesday, Friday, 3.00-5.00; Squadron K, Tuesday, Thursday, 1.00-3.00; Squadron L, Monday, Wednesday, Friday, 1.00-3.00.

are used also by a party traveling the length of a trench for the purpose of clearing it of the enemy, being thrown over each traverse approached before the party ventures around the corner. In consideration of the latter fact, the form adopted has emphasized the necessity of swinging the arm uniformly in the vertical plane. The elbow is kept straight and the grenade sent spiraling, as in a long forward pass with an American football. Since many types of grenades must be percussed before throwing and must not be dropped after the percussing has been done, the form requires that the grenade be watched constantly from the moment of percussion so that the hand will not strike unseen objects. The free hand is held horizontally forward and the corresponding foot placed forward in the same vertical plane, both pointing in the direction of the throw.

As the purpose in throwing the grenade is to drop it into a trench or hole, a direct horizontal throw is not desirable, for the grenade so thrown would pass over the trench or rebound from the embankment in front of it. Practice, therefore, aims first to develop a proper *form* and a *methodical procedure,* and then, accuracy in judging distance and in lobbing or tossing the grenade over distances varying from a few yards to forty or fifty yards in extent.

### Drills.

I. Standing Throw.

1. Advance the left (or right) foot about 24 inches. Extend the left hand, pointing same in direction of throw. Carry the grenade forward in right hand, holding it crosswise of the right palm, thumb circling grenade, and, leaning forward with body, tap grenade on palm of the left hand at the command, FIRE! (see Figure 1), and immediately swing the arm up and back in the vertical plane, following it with the eyes till the arm is extended backward and obliquely downward, body leaning well back, right leg bent. (See Figure 2.) Execute the throw from this position by carrying the grenade up and over the head, elbow straight, arm moving in the *vertical* plane. (See Figure 3.)

2. *Forward to position,* MARCH! *Prepare to throw,* FIRE! Attention! etc.

3. The chief difficulty experienced in teaching grenade throwing is that of developing the straight arm throw with arm moving in the *vertical plane.* This may be accomplished by frequent and careful drill in bringing the arm from the rear to a vertical position beside the head until this coördination is thoroughly mastered; also by having the men throw over a horizontal bar about 7 feet 6 inches high, directly above their heads; or, better still, from a cage of three walls of the above height, dimensions 6 feet by 5 feet, simulating more exactly trench conditions as to cramped throwing space.

FIG. 1.—First position: Exercise I—Throw-Standing. Percussion of the grenade; left hand and left foot are pointed toward the objective to give direction to the vertical plane of the throw.

FIG. 2.—Second position: Exercise I—Throw-Standing. The body lies in a vertical plane with the left side toward the objective. The eyes follow the grenade.

FIG. 3.—Third position: Exercise I—Throw-Standing. The delivery; the arm is carried forward in the vertical plane, weight shifted forward to aid in the throw. Note that the grenade is rolled from the hand to cause it to spiral as it flies on its way.

II. Kneeling Throw.

1. Advance left foot and arm, as in Exercise I, and kneel on right knee, lower leg being placed at right angles to direction of fire. Proceed as in Exercise I, rising from knee slightly as throw is executed, thus utilizing strength of right leg in throwing. For 2 and 3, see Exercise I.

III. Throw from Lying Position.

1. Lying on ground, head and left hand pointing in direction of fire, left leg drawn up, proceed as in 1 of Exercise I, rising slightly on left hand and left leg and foot as right hand goes back for throw. For 2 and 3, see Exercise I.

## BOXING.

The following boxing drills are offered as a result of several years' experience in the teaching of college men to fight with their fists, by means of the mass-drill method.

Experience has led to the conviction that by the method outlined as large a number of men as can be reached by the voice can be trained as one man in efficient fist-fighting. In the cramped space of the university boxing room, 30 feet by 80 feet, fifty men can be maneuvered at one time in such mass drill.

In spite of the skepticism of professional coaches as to the possibility of developing real fighting skill through such methods, this work has justified itself beyond question. As an athletic sport it is now the most extensively patronized of any of the fifteen sports offered at the University of California, and the University has been highly successful in intercollegiate competition in boxing as a result of this method of mass training.

This instruction in boxing is now being required by government authorities as a phase of the preliminary training for the eighty naval preparation students stationed at the University of California and for the eight hundred and fifty student aviators in the University School of Military Aeronautics.

The following methods of teaching boxing and the employment of boxing for the purpose of physical education are justifiable from four points of view:

In the *first* place, the method makes possible the instruction of large masses of men in a most interesting and practical form of athletics.

In the *second* place, this method of teaching boxing develops a cool and thoughtful attitude of mind, for each man comes to realize, through drill, that his opponent is expected to hit a certain definite blow and hit it hard, and that he, in his turn, is expected to block or slip this particular punch in a definite way; and he therefore realizes that in case he gets hurt he has only himself to blame. The natural outcome therefore is that each man finds it necessary to study his own faults of defense rather than waste time and energy seeking revenge by slugging. The attitude of mind thus developed should have a most important influence over the psychosis and spirit of the boxing room; blood may be expected to flow freely in every class, but "bad blood" need never be seen, as hard hitting is in compliance with orders, and the man under the necessity of serving as a punching dummy for his partner for periods of two or three minutes at a stretch and having definite instructions not to hit back, or at best to hit only a certain blow as a counter, soon gets the habit of self-control and of studying and perfecting his own faults of defense, and forgets to *get mad*. Thus a man's mind centers largely upon himself under the punishment experienced later in real competition; and his attack becomes calculated, without rancor, and therefore efficient.

A *third* valuable result of this type of training is the development of morale and self-confidence, especially noticeable among those men who formerly have been unaccustomed, in their coddled experience, to hard knocks of any kind. The soft, effeminate, even frail type of youth, gets a new light in his eyes as he finds that his moral courage, reacting to this sort of training, can "stand the gaff," and that he is gaining practical power and ability as his muscles grow and harden in the process of physical training.

The *last*, but not the least, of the great values accruing from this class drill in clean-cut, scientific fist-fighting is the physical training involved. No one can doubt the physiological values accomplished in the boxing drill, for they are clearly self-evident. Since acquiring the art of boxing involves the development of powers of balance, agility, accuracy of muscular coördination and instantaneous judgments, combined with a sympathetic, supple activity of the entire muscular system, it is readily seen that this exercise is calculated to train its devotee to meet most of the physical exigencies of life, and therefore provide him with an excellent physical education.

The style of fighting taught in the following drills is the calculating, open, or "spider" type, with straight, hard punching, and a minimum of the milling, hooking, clinching tactics favored largely by the mediocre prize-ring artists. It is the type perfection in which requires years of practice, and is best exemplified in the fighting of such men as Corbett, Fitzsimmons, Ritchie, Leonard, O'Brien, and Gans. In the actual competition, which should at first be very limited as to duration and should follow directly after each class drill, men should be instructed, observed, and advised personally as to the best methods of adapting the fundamentals learned to their individual aptitudes for infighting, blocking, etc.

The drills should be organized as nearly as possible in keeping with military procedure, since it is recognized that methods which have proved especially efficient in the military maneuvering of large groups of men must be good educational procedure for any drill work. Thus the class is divided into units or platoons, marched to place and finally arranged in two ranks, men in both ranks facing to the front during the *shadow boxing,* but with the front rank facing the rear rank for the *opposition drills.*

### Shadow Boxing—Fundamental Positions.

I. On Guard.

1. Advance the left foot 18 to 20 inches to the front, keeping the weight on the ball of the right foot, right heel slightly raised, right toe pointed obliquely forward, right knee slightly bent, feet spread and so placed that they occupy *diagonally opposite corners* of a 14-inch square placed at right angles to a line drawn between the opponents; body erect, facing three-quarters front. Direct left toe toward opponent's right foot, and left hand at opponent's jaw, bending arm to an angle of 135° at the elbow, and carrying the entire arm in the vertical plane, palm of hand turned up and fingers relaxed. Hold right hand with palm toward opponent, tips of fingers about height of chin, with arm bent to an angle of 45° at the elbow and with the elbow and upper arm held *close to the body.* Keep left shoulder about 6 inches higher than right and draw in neck, turtlelike, tucking chin close to chest. (See Figure 4.)

2. *On* GUARD! ATTENTION! etc.

3. It is important that the novice follow directions closely as to detail of position and acquire habits of assuming and maintaining these positions subconsciously. The positions given are slightly exaggerated, but this is necessary to overcome the natural tendencies to assume positions simulating the above but lacking in actual power and protective value. It is very important that the left arm be held in the *vertical* plane, thus bringing the elbow well in front, protecting the body and insuring the ultimate development of a powerful straight-left punch; also, that the palm of the left hand be *turned up,* as this forces the arm to lie in the *vertical plane.* The right hand must be held with the palm forward, thus bringing the *soft pad* of the glove against the face, and both hands should be open and relaxed, and the entire body as relaxed as possible, since a contracted, stiff position results in slow, inefficient action. Holding the left shoulder *high,* the chin *low,* elbows close to body, are most important sources of defense against the deadly right cross. The body must be carried with the shoulders turned squarely to the front—a line drawn through the shoulders should be maintained very nearly at right angles

FIG. 4.—On-Guard Position. Right elbow close to body, left elbow and arm in vertical plane, weight on right toe, left leg set, body three-fourths square to the front with the feet spread to the sides. See Exercise I.

FIG. 5.—Right Hand and Elbow Block; for straight left jab. Note position of the chin, right hand and elbow. See Exercise II.

FIG. 6.—Left-Hand and Elbow Block. Ready to deliver the right to head or body. See Exercise III.

FIG. 7.—Safety Block. Both Hands and Elbows. Note position of the hands and elbows. Eyes peek between the hands to determine the position of opponent. See Exercise IV.

to a line drawn from one opponent to the other. This square-to-the-front position is absolutely necessary to the development of *skill* and *power*.

It is extremely important that the left toe be pointed directly at the opponent, for this position is vital to the *maintenance of balance* in delivering a hard punch with either hand.

Practice in assuming this position should be continued until each man has mastered it, as otherwise practice in the more advanced drills or in boxing will only accentuate bad habits that may prove disastrous later in competition.

When the assuming of this position has become subconscious, the individual may drop the hands for rest when at a safe distance, but should assume the position again instantly when nearing the danger zone.

II. Block. *Right Hand, Elbow and Shoulder.*

1. Press the padded side of the right glove close against the left side of the head as the latter is turned slightly to the right, chin tucked firmly against the chest. Keep the right forearm and elbow pressed close against the body, elbow well forward, and at the same time brace the right hand against the left shoulder, which in turn should be raised about 6 inches and thrust forward momentarily, to take or help break the force of the opponent's punch. (See Figure 5.)

2. *Block position, right hand,* PLACE! ATTENTION! etc.

3. See Exercise I. Jaws should be firmly locked and neck muscles taut at the moment when blow is received, and the body should be flexible and yielding as the blow is received unless a counter is being delivered.

III. Block. *Left Hand and Elbow.*

1. Hold pad of left glove against right ear as the head is turned to the left and bend the body forward and slightly to the left, head down as far as possible in the crotch of the left elbow. Tuck the chin into the chest and hold the left elbow far enough from the body to bring it opposite the eyebrows and thus protect the face. (See Figure 6.)

2. *Block position, left hand,* PLACE! ATTENTION! etc.

IV. Block. *Both Hands and Elbows.*

1. Press padded side of each glove against its respective side of the forehead, leaning slightly forward with the face covered, and in this manner hold the elbows close against the body and about 5 inches apart. Watch opponent from between the gloves, chin tucked close to the chest. (See Figure 7.)

2. *Block, both hands, forearms vertical,* PLACE! ATTENTION! etc.

3. See Exercise I. This "block" should be assumed only when overcrowded or fatigued, and the fighter should never emerge from behind the gloves until distance from the opponent has been gained or until aggressive tactics may immediately be resorted to. Eyes must be kept on opponent.

V. Advance. *On-Guard Position.*

1. Advance left foot 12 to 14 inches, keeping the body weight on the ball of the right foot, right heel slightly raised; slip right foot forward *instantly* to *maintain original "On-Guard" position.* Face squarely to the front at all times. Repeat to command or in series.

2. *On* GUARD! ADVANCE! ADVANCE! HALT! ATTENTION! etc.; or, in series, class continuing to execute each maneuver until new one is called for. ADVANCE! RETREAT! *Side step,* LEFT! etc. HALT! ATTENTION!

3. The body from hips up should be immobile and turned *squarely front* throughout the exercise. The weight should rest *chiefly* on the *right foot.* In short the fundamental on-guard position should be maintained while advancing or retreating, but care must be taken to avoid a stiff or contracted condition of body and arms. The action of the body and feet should be like that seen in a good dancer: lithe, supple, and easy. The right foot must follow the left instantly, making the movement of the two feet almost as simultaneous as in a jump. The action must be smooth, however.

VI. Retreat. *On-Guard Position.*

1. Slide right foot back 12 to 14 inches and follow immediately with the left foot, thus constantly maintaining the *relative position* of the feet, and holding the body ready to attack, retreat, or resist attack, at any instant. Repeat to command or in series.

2. *On* GUARD! RETREAT! RETREAT! ADVANCE! *Side step,* etc. See Exercise I.

3. Note carefully Exercise I.

VII. Side step. *On-Guard Position.*

1. Step about 16 inches to the left with the left foot or to the right with the right foot, and follow immediately with the opposite foot, keeping feet always in the same *relative position.*

2. *On* GUARD! *Side step,* LEFT! LEFT! RIGHT! LEFT! ADVANCE! RETREAT! or in series. See Part 2, Exercise V.

For 3, note carefully Exercise I.

VIII. Straight-Left Jab to Head. *On-Guard Position.*

1. Step forward as explained in Exercise V and simultaneously extend the left arm, carrying it throughout in the vertical plane, thus developing a pistonlike action and landing the fist squarely on the opponent's blocking glove or jaw, with a slight upward drive. At the same instant throw into the punch the power of the triggerlike right leg—carried forward in the advance to *anticipate* the blow—and the power of the pivoting muscles of the waist and shoulders, turning from the "square-to-the-front position" to a position with the left shoulder directed toward the opponent as the blow is delivered. Block with the right hand, as directed in Exercise II. (See Figure 8.)

2. *On* GUARD! *Rank No. 1, strike left to the jaw; Rank No. 2, block with right hand,* STEP! or CHARGE! RETREAT! etc. Or, again, *Rank No. 1, strike left to the jaw and block with the right; Rank No. 2, block with the right and counter with the left to head or body,* STEP! etc.

3. Consider carefully Exercise I. In striking this, as well as other blows, with either right or left hand, the body *should not lean forward,* and the force of the blow should result from the combined power of right leg, arm, shoulder, and pivoting waist and chest muscles. Leaning forward will shift the body weight to the left foot, thus slowing foot action, or will even carry the weight beyond the support of the left leg, thus destroying the balance and making impossible a series of two or more punches. Leaning forward is one of the most dangerous tendencies the boxer must combat and one of the most difficult to overcome, as it naturally results from his attempt to gain distance and to lend power to his punch. The only way to overcome this tendency is to step in deep, carrying the weight well back on the right foot. Practice in executing blows before a mirror or in striking a bag filled with bran having a central core of sand to give it weight is most valuable. All blows should be practiced without an opponent at first, then with a passive opponent, next with an opponent executing a definite counter, and finally studied with reference to time, distance, and speed in actual combat. In striking any blow the fist should be clinched only at the instant of delivering the blow, and the end of the fist should meet the impact with the thumb held close, and the back of the hand in line with the forearm. The command STEP or CHARGE is given instead of HIT, etc., to prompt the use of the feet, since the most important accomplishment of a skilled boxer—and the most difficult thing for the novice to learn—is this ability to "step in." The "step in" at the instant of striking is necessary in gaining distance and in adding the force of the body's momentum to the power of the punch. Straight punching is emphasized, as it is the most difficult to master and the most valuable in practical application. The hooks and swings come only too naturally to most, and skill in their

use will develop naturally in connection with competition as proficiency is gained in balance and footwork. If the command RETREAT is not given, it is to be understood that retreat should follow immediately on delivery of a blow or combination of blows, and that the blocking position is to be maintained until a safe distance has been gained. Great care should be taken not to form

FIG. 8.—Straight-Left Jab to Head. Note erect position of body which has been pivoted as right leg straightens to give force to the blow. Chin is drawn close, head slightly turned and tilted, right elbow held close, right hand pressed against left shoulder to resist shock of encounter. See Exercise VIII.

FIG. 9.—Delivery of left jab to the body as a counter for a left jab to the face, the latter being slipped over the left shoulder of the figure to the right. Note the drive coming from the right toe, right leg being fully extended as the blow is landed. See Exercise IX.

habits of drawing back the fist just before hitting as valuable time is thus lost, vulnerable spots exposed, and advance information as to punches telegraphed to the opponent.

IX. Straight-Left Jab to Body. *On-Guard Position.*

1. Proceed exactly as described in Exercise VIII, save that the blow is delivered over the heart or in the median line just below the ribs. See 2 and 3, Exercise VIII. (See Figure 9.)

X. Straight-Right to Head. *On-Guard Position.*

1. Step close to opponent as described in Exercise V and simultaneously extend the right arm, carrying the right fist in a *direct line* from its resting place (see "On-Guard Position") to the jaw of opponent, pivoting to the left to bring right shoulder forward, and at the same time drop the head to the left into the shelter of the left-hand-and-elbow block (see Exercise II).

2. On GUARD! *Rank No. 1, strike right to the jaw; Rank No. 2, block right hand, elbow and shoulder,* BLOCK! etc.; or, *counter left to jaw,* etc.—for the particular combination desired—STEP! or CHARGE! RETREAT! etc.

3. Note carefully Exercise VIII. In delivering this blow, turn the body as on a *vertical pivot* and at the same time throw the full power of the right leg into the punch. It is most difficult to execute this blow without losing power in the vain attempt to gain it by swinging the arm instead of making a straight drive. The blow should be executed with a lifting impact and the tendency to "hammer," or to bring the fist first up and then down in the delivery, must be overcome. In actual contest this punch is best executed as a counter, following a left lead or feint. Every boxer has certain eccentricities through which he telegraphs his punches to a greater or less extent, and ability to read these and calculate time and distance correctly should be the ambition of every boxer. With this ability he can "slip" the punches of his opponent and take advantage of the latter's momentum in giving power to his own blows at the same time that he gains access to the vulnerable spots of his opponent, which must be exposed more or less in any attack.

XI. Straight-Right to Body. *On-Guard Position.*

1. Proceed exactly as directed in Exercise X. Seek the objectives described in Exercise IX. See 2 and 3, Exercises VIII and X.

## GENERAL METHODS OF CLASS DRILL.

### Drills.

XII. Shadow Boxing Drill.

1. Form class in company front. Demand close attention to military procedure in respect to snappy response to commands and to position throughout the drill with reference to the class as a whole. Maintain straight lines front and rear, left and right, as far as possible. Give the command "Cover" and "*Guide* Right" after each series of movements and thus train the class to react in orderly fashion and in unison.

2. *At two paces, take distance,* MARCH! HALT! COVER! GUIDE RIGHT! *On* GUARD! ADVANCE! ADVANCE! ADVANCE! RETREAT! RETREAT! RETREAT! *Side step,* LEFT! RIGHT! LEFT! etc.; *Straight-left to face or body,* HIT! HIT! HIT! ADVANCE! ADVANCE! LEFT! RIGHT! HIT! HIT! RETREAT! HIT! LEFT! etc.

3. The above drill should be varied after a few minutes of practice by instructing class to continue the movement called for by the command "Advance" until the second movement is called for by the command "Hit," "Retreat" or "Left," thus passing from one phase of the drill to another with the class continually in action. The command "Hit" should be followed by a pause to insure the development of balance control. The instructor will find it necessary to analyze the straight-left jab as described in Exercise VIII. This may be done by a drill demanding the execution of the "straight-left jab" to two commands, namely, "Step" and "Hit." On the first command each man steps one pace, as described in the advance under Exercise V, maintaining his "on-guard" position until the command "Hit" is given, when the blow is executed with careful attention to proper weight distribution and position of elbows, hands, and feet. The man must assume the "on-guard" position instantly after hitting the imaginary opponent. Such drill is valuable in training the novice to avoid leaning forward in the delivery of the punch, the instructor constantly insisting on the development of the pivot movement and the right-leg drive, as described in Exercise VIII.

XIII. Opposition Drill. *Straight-Left and Right-Hand Block.*

1. Form class in company front (two ranks). Have men take distance to side at single arm's length. Face front rank to the rear and direct men to return to and maintain proper distance whenever not actually engaged in hitting. Urge careful attention to positions, weight distribution and form in hitting, as described under Exercises II, V, VIII, etc.

2. *Company or Squadron,* ATTENTION! *Take distance at arm's length guiding right, left or center,* MARCH! *Front rank about,* FACE! *On* GUARD! *Front rank advance one pace at the command "step,"* STEP! *Strike straight-left to opponent's jaw, block with the right hand and immediately retreat one pace; rear rank stand fast, block with right hand, counter with the left, striking straight-left jab to number one's jaw,* HIT! HIT! STEP! HIT! STEP! etc. After brief drill on elements of blow instruct class to execute all three elements, "step in," "hit" and "retreat" to the one command "Step." *On* GUARD! STEP! STEP! etc.; then reverse the order (rear rank attacks, front rank counters); and, finally, ATTENTION! *At* EASE!; or *front rank about,* FACE! etc.

3. The same method of drill can be used in teaching each of

the leads and blocks described above and the various counters to be used. The instructor should constantly urge attention to weight distribution, positions of feet, hands and body, and to the proper execution of blows. In these drills the habits are being formed which will determine skilled or unskilled performance later in serious competition.

XIV. Opposition Drill. *Series of Punches.*

1. Proceed as in Exercise XIII.
2. Proceed as in Exercise XIII and continue: *Front rank step in and strike left to opponent's jaw on the command "Step" and without retreating pass instantly from right-hand block to left-hand block and deliver right to opponent's head (or body). Rear rank men assume proper head- (or body) blocking position and counter with straight-left to head (or body) or assume safety block (Exercise IV) and accept the "punishment,"* STEP! STEP! etc.; then REVERSE the order, etc.
3. In similar fashion a series of three or more punches may be executed to command, one rank aggressing, the other rank blocking and countering. Also, according to definite directions, the front rank men may strike left to opponent's jaw, right to body, left-hook to jaw, and get away, to definite commands, or to count, "1, 2, 3, 4," and so on in great variety, insisting always that good habits be developed by proper observance of form in the process of such drills.

## STRUGGLING EXERCISES—IN COUPLES.

I. Pushing.

1. A and B attempt to push each other across a given line, each grasping opponent's shoulders with hands.
2. *To position,* MARCH! On Guard, GO! HALT! ATTENTION! *Next squad or rank to position,* MARCH! etc.
3. Same type of exercise can be accomplished by A and B grasping opposite ends of a short pole. Contests should be of short duration—30 seconds at first—and gradually increasing in severity.

II. Pulling.

1. A and B attempt to pull each other across a line by grasping arms.
2. See Exercise I.
3. Same type of exercise can be accomplished by A and B grasping hands, wrists (as in forming a seat), rope, or pole, or varied by using one hand instead of two. For duration see 3, Exercise I.

III. Wrestling for Possession of Gun, Caps, or Staff.

1. A and B grasp the same gun or staff, each having one hand in upper and the other in reverse grip. Each attempts to wrest the gun or staff from the opponent's hands.

2 and 3. See Exercise I.

IV. Advantage Wrestling.

1. A and B each attempt to get behind opponent's back and in that position grasp him firmly about the waist, which accomplishment constitutes a fall.

2. *To position,* MARCH! *Prepare to wrestle,* GO!

3. Men should not fall to the ground in this contest. See Exercise I.

V. Westmoreland Wrestling.

1. A and B each attempt to cause opponent to touch three points to the ground by throwing him off his balance. (Two feet and one hand, two feet and one knee, two hands and one foot, etc., touching the ground constitute a fall.)

2. *To position,* MARCH! *Prepare to wrestle,* GO! ATTENTION! etc. For 3, see Exercise I.

VI. Japanese Wrestling.

1. A and B attempt to cause opponent to leave ring 12 feet in diameter. One foot on or across line constitutes a fall. For 2, see Exercise V.

VII. Hand Wrestling.

1. A and B stand side by side facing in opposite directions, grasping inside hands. Each contestant attempts to cause opponent to lose his balance and move either foot. For 2, see Exercise V and Figure 11.

3. Feet to the inside should be touching; moving either foot from starting position constitutes a fall. For duration, see Exercise I.

VIII. Indian Wrestling.

1. A and B lie on the ground face up, shoulder to shoulder, inside arms locked, feet extending in opposite directions. The inside legs (outside may be used) are simultaneously brought to the vertical position to count and on the third count the feet, ankles and legs are entwined in an effort to cause the opponent to execute a back roll.

2. *To position,* MARCH! *Prepare to wrestle,* ONE, TWO, THREE! ATTENTION!

Fig. 11.—Class Drill in hand wrestling, University of California campus. December 1, 1917. See Exercise VII—Struggling Exercises.

## LIFTING AND CARRYING EXERCISES.

I. Four-Men Carry.

1. A, B, C and D carry E, eight hands interlaced to form a hammock for E to lie in.
2. *To position,* MARCH! *Prepare to carry, forward,* MARCH! HALT! DOWN! ATTENTION! etc.
3. Platoons may be pitted against each other in relay contests of various sorts, in which case only an initial command should be given.

II. Two-Men Carry.

1. A and B carry C; A takes C's legs at knees, one under each arm, his back turned to C's head; B grasps C under arms about chest. For 2 and 3, see Exercise I.

III. Two-Men Carry.

1. A and B carry C, either inside or outside arms of A and B interlaced to form seat for C. For 2 and 3, see Exercise I.

IV. Two-Men Carry.

1. A and B carry C, four hands of A and B interlaced to form seat for C. For 2 and 3, see Exercise I.

V. One-Man Front Carry.

1. A carries B, placing right arm under B's left and about his chest, B throwing right arm over A's shoulder and clinging there; A's left arm crossing above B's right side and down about B's knees, holding latter close to A's body. For 2, see Exercise I.
3. Men should be well matched as to weight so as not to overstrain. Carrying should be for very short distances at first.

VI. One-Man Front Carry.

1. A carries B, right hand and forearm below B's knees, left hand passed behind B's back and about his waist, both arms thus under and on the same side of B who hangs limp, face up. For 2, see Exercise I; for 3, see Exercise II.

VII. One-Man Back Carry.

1. A carries B sitting on A's shoulders, legs straddling A's neck, B's ankles grasped by A's hands.
2. *To position,* MARCH! UP! *Forward,* MARCH! HALT! DOWN! ATTENTION! etc. For 3, see Exercise III and Exercise V.

VIII. One-Man Back Carry.

1. A carries B, whose legs straddle A's back just above the hips, where they are supported by A's hands or forearms, while B's arms hang over or grasp A's shoulders. For 2, see Exercise VII; for 3, see Exercise V.

IX. One-Man Single-Shoulder Carry.

1. A carries B thrown over one shoulder like a sack of grain, stomach down and head forward, A's shoulder at B's hip joint. For 2, see Exercise I.
3. This carry may be executed also with B's head to the rear. In assuming position to undertake carry, A should squat in front of B, either facing to or from him, according to the carry to be executed.

X. One-Man Double-Shoulder Carry.

1. A faces B, grasping B's right wrist in his right hand. A leans forward, passes to the outside of B's right arm, turns to the right and passes head and shoulders under B's right arm, with his back turned to B, and, at the same time passing his left arm through B's crotch, rises to a standing position firmly grasping B's left leg and drawing B's body close against his shoulders, with

B's waist directly behind his head. A's left arm can then be extended to grasp B's right or left wrist, thus freeing A's right hand for climbing purposes. For 2, see Exercise I. (See Figure 12.)

Fig. 12.—Relay Race; Double-Shoulder Carry. See Exercise X—Carrying Exercises.

3. Same carry can be executed by A passing arms about both of B's legs and grasping B's neck when body is finally in position on shoulders. If man is properly balanced it is even possible to free both hands for climbing purposes:

XI. One-Man Lift. *Shouldering a Limp and Unconscious Body.*

1. A turns B (limp and unconscious on the ground) face down and, standing at his head, places his hands under B's shoulders, raises him just enough to permit the placing of his (A's) left knee under B's chest. From this position A places both arms around B under his arms and lifts him enough to permit placing the left knee between B's legs. A then takes B's left hand in his right and places his head under B's left arm, at the same time slipping his own left arm between B's legs and, grasping B's left leg, pulls B's weight upon his shoulders. A then takes B's left wrist in his left hand leaving his right hand free to assist in rising. For 2, see Exercise I. (See Figure 13.)

3. Care should be taken in pairing off men so that no one will be called upon at first, to lift more than his own weight.

Fig. 13.—Positions 1, 2 and 3. Lifting the limp or unconscious person from the ground to position for a double-shoulder carry. See Exercise XI—Lifting and Carrying Exercises.

XII. One-Man Lift. *Arm and Knee Lock.*\*

1. A turns B face up upon the ground with arms at his sides and kneels at B's left side (his right knee close to B's hip): A then lifts B's knees well up and toward his (B's) head placing his own left knee under B's knees. From this position A shifts B's knees to his left shoulder and upper arm, reaching around the thighs with his left hand and firmly grasping B's left wrist. A places his head under B's left arm (being careful to shift the arm well toward the base of the neck rather than close to the head) and straightens, B's body being drawn upward upon A's right thigh. With his right hand, A shifts B's weight to his (A's) left knee (as far as possible from the body). From this position, with the assistance of his right hand, A rises to a standing position, lifting B as high as possible.

2. See Exercise XI.

3. A man should not be called upon to lift more than his own weight at first. After practice, a man weighing 135 pounds should be able to lift and carry one weighing 160 pounds.

XIII. Lifting, Carrying, and Tossing Sacks of Different Weights.

1. See medicine ball exercises.

General Comment: Various sports, such as cock fights, relays, climbing contests, etc., can be developed in connection with the various carrying exercises. Care should be taken, however, not to overdo by too long or too severe tests.

## SCALING EXERCISES.

### Ladder Scaling.

I. Ladder Scaling, Vertical Position, Top Side.

1. Mount ladder, hands on beams; same, with hands on rungs.
2. *To position*, MARCH! *Prepare to climb*, UP! HALT! DOWN! ATTENTION! etc.

II. Ladder Scaling, Oblique Position, Top Side.

1. Mount ladder, body vertical, without use of hands, arms in the horizontal-side position, to aid in balancing. For 2, see Exercise I.

III. Drag-Climb, Oblique Position, Top Side.

1. With body in front-lying position, feet dragging on beams, grasp rungs and mount ladder. For 2, see Exercise I.

---

\*As described by Capt. Howard C. Naffziger, M. R. C. The Military Surgeon. April, 1918, pp. 463-5.

IV. Ladder Scaling, Oblique Position, Under Side.

1. Mount ladder, grasping beams or rungs from below, feet placed on rungs. For 2, see Exercise I.

V. Ladder Scaling, Oblique Position, Under Side.

1. Grasp beams and, with body in suspension, mount ladder by advancing hands alternately. For 2, see Exercise I.

### Rope Climbing.

VI. Rope Climbing, "Sailor's Climb."

1. Grasp rope with both hands. Flex arms, lift body, and raise knees as high as possible, grasping rope firmly between the knees and between the ankles. Extend knees and thighs, at the same time climbing hand over hand to full extension of arms. Repeat. For 2, See Exercise I.

VII. Rope Climbing, Rest Method.

1. Proceed as in Exercise VI save that the rope is grasped only between feet. Rope should hang between knees, but should pass to the outside of one foot—say the left—and be drawn under same by the opposite or right foot crossing the instep of the right upon which it can be held firmly by standing upon the right with the left. For 2, see Exercise I.

3. This method of holding the rope is used in resting, sometimes combined with a double twist of rope about the leg or the foot, as above.

VIII. Rope Climbing, Hand Over Hand.

1. Raise body until arms are completely flexed, legs hanging free. Holding position by means of one arm, advance opposite hand 6 or 8 inches and lift body as high as possible. Repeat. For 2, see Exercise I.

### Shelf Scaling.

IX. Shelf Scaling in Pairs.—*Platform Eight Feet High.*

1. A steps into interlaced hands of B, who boosts him to shelf. B then jumps, grasping edge of shelf and lifting weight with arms as in chinning. A stands on shelf, catching B by head, and assisting him to mount. Dismount by lying prone on shelf, body from hips forward projecting beyond edge, hands grasping edge of shelf with reverse grip, and then turning forward to a hanging position and dropping thence to the ground. Repeat, reversing the order of procedure. (See Figure 14.)

2. *To position,* MARCH! *Prepare to mount,* UP! ATTENTION! *Prepare to dismount,* DOWN! OFF!

3. Care should be taken when men are dismounting to have an assistant under each man to catch him in case of accident.

FIG. 14.—Position assumed in dismount described in Scaling Exercises, Exercise IX, and in the mount described in Exercise XIV.

FIG. 15.—Shelf Scaling. Either elbow may be advanced over the edge of the shelf to assist in the mount. See Exercise X.

X. Scaling Shelf Singly, One Arm and One Leg Leading.

1. Grasp edge of shelf, lifting weight and hooking left (or right) leg over the edge. Develop momentum by diagonally swinging opposite leg downward and mount shelf assuming position of attention. About face to left or right, dropping to a hanging position. (See Figure 15.)

2. *To position*, MARCH! *Prepare to mount*, UP! ATTENTION! *Prepare to dismount from sitting position, left (or right)*, FACE! DOWN!

3. Repeat, using opposite leg. Added momentum in mounting can be gained by pushing away from shelf with lower foot.

XI. Scaling Shelf Singly, One Arm Leading.

1. Grasp edge of shelf, lift body quickly, raising right (or left) arm above level of shelf. Follow with opposite arm, pushing up to front-rest. Mount, left or right, to position of attention. For 2 and 3, see Exercise IX.

XII. Scaling Shelf Singly, with Both Arms.

1. Grasp edge of shelf and mount as in XI, bringing both arms simultaneously to the bent-arm position above the edge of the shelf, to a front-rest. Mount, left or right, to a position of attention. For 2, see Exercise XI.

XIII. Scaling Shelf Singly, by Means of the Chest Heave.

1. Grasp edge of shelf and mount as in Exercise XII, save that momentum is gained in mounting by raising the legs forward and then violently snapping to the rear with extreme arching of the back. Repeat movement until sufficient momentum has been acquired to assist in bringing arms above shelf. For 2, see Exercise XI.

XIV. Scaling Shelf Singly, by Means of the Front Pull-Up.

1. Stand under edge of shelf, facing out. Jump to hang with reverse grasp, raising legs quickly and shooting over edge of shelf to a prone position. Rise to position of attention. For 2, see Exercise XI.

3. The body should be drawn well upon the shelf before attempting to rise.

## BALANCING EXERCISES.

### Balancing on Fence Rail.

#### Exercise I.

1. Mount fence by hand vault to a straddle-sitting position, supporting weight with hands. Balancing in this position, raise legs forward and swing to a standing position.

2. *To position,* MARCH! *Prepare to vault, left (or right),* UP! *Legs,* FRONT! *To stand,* UP! *Right (or left),* FACE! DOWN!

3. Care should be taken in vaulting to rail to support weight with hands. Standing position should be held until balance can be maintained.

### Exercise II.

1. Mount fence to a side-sitting position, facing either side. Balance and turn to front-rest. Mount, left or right, to a standing position.

2. *To position,* MARCH! *Prepare to vault to left or right side-seat,* UP! *Front-rest, left (or right) about,* FACE! *Left (or right),* UP! DOWN!

### Exercise III.

1. Mount rail as in Exercise I or II. Stand on rail, balancing on both feet, arms or hands in turn to side-horizontal, vertical, shoulders, rear-of-head, thrust, strike or hips position, body inclined forward. Repeat, body inclined backward. Repeat, balancing on one foot.

2. See Exercises I or II.

3. Walk forward and then backward along bar, arms and hands taking the various starting positions designated.

## Ground Balancing.

### Exercise IV.

1. Raise left leg slowly forward and bring arms to the front-horizontal position, count, 1; move arms and leg to the side in the horizontal plane, 2; return, 3, 4.

2. *Raise,* FRONT! SIDE! FRONT! DOWN! or *to count,* 1! 2! etc.

3. Repeat three times with each leg. To get the muscular training desired from balance exercises, these should be executed slowly and on the word of command, holding momentarily the positions assumed.

### Exercise V.

1. Rise on the toes and lift the arms to the vertical position, 1; bend the knees slowly, 2; return, 3, 4.

2. *On toes,* UP! BEND! UP! DOWN! or *to count,* 1! 2!

3. Repeat three times. Arms and trunk should remain in a straight line, knees turned out; body lowered to a sitting position on heels. To increase difficulty, look at finger tips when at full knee-bend position. See Exercise I.

### Exercise VI.

1. Bend arms to thrust and flex left knee, 1; extend arms and leg forward, 2; return, 3, 4.
2. *Arms,* BEND! EXTEND! BEND! DOWN! or *to count,* 1! 2! etc.
3. Repeat left and right three times. Insist on good positions and balance. See Exercise I.

### Exercise VII.

1. Bend arms to thrust and flex left knee, 1; extend leg to rear and arms over head, lowering trunk forward to the horizontal plane, 2; return, 3, 4.
2. *Arms,* BEND! EXTEND! BEND! DOWN! or *to count,* 1! 2! etc.
3. Repeat left and right three times. In the second movement the arms, body and leg should be in one horizontal line. See Exercise I.

### Exercise VIII.

1. Lunge forward to the left extending the left arm forward and oblique-upward, the right down and oblique-backward, 1; transfer the weight to the left leg by raising the right leg backward and, at the same time, straighten the left knee and change arm positions, right up and left down, 2; return, 3, 4.
2. *Lunge,* LEFT! UP! DOWN! POSITION! or *to count,* 1! 2! 3! 4!
3. Repeat left and right three times. See Exercise I.

## JUMPING AND VAULTING EXERCISES.

### Jumping Exercises.

I. Standing Broad Jump.

1. Squat to the full-bend position, arms extended in the front-horizontal. Swing arms downward to the rear and then forward *stopping in the bent-arm position,* thus adding the momentum of the swinging arms as the body leaves the ground.
2. *To position,* MARCH! *Prepare to jump,* JUMP!
3. The knees should be lifted high and the body turned slightly to one side in landing in order to gain distance. A string or rope extended in front of jumpers will aid in gaining proper height.

II. Standing High Jump.

1. Same as the above, save that energy of the spring is directed upward instead of forward. For 2 and 3, see Exercise I.

III. Standing Broad-and-High Dive.

1. Assume same position as in Exercise I. Spring into the air as high as possible, developing a rotary momentum by causing the body to describe an arc in the dive to the ground, feet thrown high. Catch the weight in landing with the arms slightly bent, muscles taut. As the hands strike the ground tuck chin close to chest and lower weight on the back of the head and shoulders, maintaining the momentum in regaining feet. For 2, see Exercise I.

3. Care should be taken to throw the feet well up in the air to insure a proper rotation as the body strikes the ground.

IV. Running Broad Jump.

1. Take off at as great speed as is conducive to accuracy in leaving the ground and in gaining the proper height in the air. Lift feet well out in front, tucking knees close to the chest. Turn slightly to one side in landing and fall forward, to gain distance.

2. *To position,* MARCH! *Prepare to run,* RUN! ATTENTION! etc.

3. Jumper should run about 30 yards to gain speed, making last three strides short and taking-off with body erect, striving to gain as much height as possible. The run should be practiced until an accurate take-off is assured.

V. Running High Jump.

1. Side, roll, or scissors. For 2 and 3, see Exercise IV.

VI. Jumping Forward and Backward to Ground from an Elevation.

1. Jump forward or backward, as in Exercise I, to the ground, landing with legs slightly bent, muscles taut, feet about 14 inches or 18 inches apart, alighting with the arms in the front-horizontal position to assist in preserving balance. For 2, see Exercise I.

3. This jump should be made first from low elevations until accuracy and proper balance have been developed.

### Vaulting Exercises.

VII. Vaulting Fence or Other Obstacles. (See Figure 16.)

1. (a) Front-vault. Cross bar face down, back arched. (b) Flank vault. Face front, side of body toward bar, back straight. (c) Rear-vault. Face to side, body in sitting position. (d) Squat-vault. Face to front, feet passing between hands. (e) Straddle-vault. Face to front, feet outside of hands. (f) Fencer's front-vault. (g) Fencer's flank-vault. (h) Fencer's rear-vault.

2. *To position,* MARCH! *Prepare to vault (left or right),* UP! ATTENTION! etc.

3. In all save the squat-vault, knees and back should be kept as straight as possible, toes pointed, head up and shoulders square. Sufficient vigor should be exerted by arms to cause body to rise well above the rail, especially in the straddle-vault. The fencer's vaults differ from a, b, c and d only in that the fence or other obstacle is approached from a left- or right-oblique position and the take-off is from one foot, and only one hand is used in support in crossing the fence.

Fig. 16.—Military drill in fence vaulting at the eucalyptus grove gymnasium of the University of California campus. Preparing to vault. See Exercise VII, Vaulting Exercises.

VIII. Vaulting to Back of Horse, and the Dismount.

1. Stand on left side of horse. Grasp imaginary reins in left hand, placing same at base of neck, grasp pommel of saddle with right hand and vault to saddle. Dismount to same side by lifting weight free of horse and dropping lightly to the ground.

2. *To position,* MARCH! *Prepare to vault,* UP! OFF! ATTENTION! etc.

IX. Pole Vault for Height.

1. If right handed, grasp pole with the right hand, knuckles down, at the point on the pole corresponding to the height to be

vaulted. Grasp the pole with the left hand about two feet below the right, knuckles up. Carry the pole at the right side, head as far forward as possible, and point of pole elevated. Run forward and drive the point of the pole into the ground at the take-off, sliding the left hand up to the right and extending both arms over the head as the body leaves the ground. Spring from the right foot, pulling up with the arms, and pass on the right side of the pole, shooting the feet high above the hands and turning face down while passing over the bar. Release pole and alight facing the bar. For 2, see Exercise IV.

3. Ability to handle the pole should be developed before attempting to gain height. A very short run should be used at first. A run of twenty yards should prove sufficient for any height. The last three strides before the take-off should be short and snappy. Pole vaulting should never be practiced unless plenty of sawdust is provided in the jumping-pit.

X. Pole Vault for Distance.

1. Same as Exercise IX, save that the pole is held throughout the jump.

NOV 4 1918

Printed by Libri Plureos GmbH in Hamburg, Germany